Chalk Full of Laughs

Chalk Full of Laughs

Hilarious Histories From the Classroom

ROBERT FAVRETTO

amba press

Published in 2025 by Amba Press, Melbourne, Australia
www.ambapress.com.au

© Robert Favretto 2025

All rights reserved. No part of this book may be reproduced or transmitted in any form or by any means, electronic or mechanical, including photocopying, recording or by any information storage and retrieval system, without prior permission in writing from the publisher.

Cover design: Tess McCabe
Internal design: Amba Press
Editor: Andrew Campbell

ISBN: 9781923403307 (pbk)
ISBN: 9781923403314 (ebk)

A catalogue record for this book is available from the National Library of Australia.

ALSO BY ROBERT FAVRETTO

A Long Way from Home

Crash Landing: Otto's Alien Adventure

Boris Goes Berserk

Morphing Murphy

Gorski's Bitemare

Home of the Cuckoo Clock

CAT-apult

CAT-astrophe

On the Nose

Leonardo's Spot of Trouble

Lost for Words

PRAISE

'This book should be required reading for all trainee teachers, to show what it means to relate to students, to hear them, to enjoy them and to see what it looks like when a good teacher brings joy to the wonderful and rewarding profession of teaching.'

– *Dr Lawrence Ingvarson AM, former Professor of Education, Monash University, and Director of Teaching and Learning, Australian Council of Educational Research*

'Robert's insightful yet piercingly humorous reflections on his years as a teacher instil an awareness of the rich tapestry of experiences the classroom offers. To Robert, the classroom, the school and the schoolyards become the cauldron of mystique, humour, and challenging uncertainty that forged him, not just as an educator, but as a human being and a storyteller.'

– *Dr Ron Wilson PSM, principal, teacher, manager and author*

'*Chalk Full of Laughs* is an absolute gem! Robert (aka Mr Fav) captures the heart and humour of classroom life with warmth, wit and charm, as he recounts his experiences as a primary school teacher during a career spanning several decades. A joyful, uplifting read, which truly honours the students that Robert taught, this book is guaranteed to leave you chuckling, reminiscing and smiling!'

– *David Provan, Former Chair of Friendly Pharmacy (Vic) Ltd and General Manager of the Adult Parole Board of Victoria*

'A wonderful collection of stories from a teaching career defined by laughter, warmth, and unforgettable highlights. With Robert's trademark humour, care and dedication to the profession, he turned classrooms into stages of fun and staffrooms into sanctuaries of friendship. For all of us lucky enough to have taught beside him, Robert was and still is the CEO of laughter, making every school day brighter for all.'

– *Steven Wishart, Principal Consultant and Child Safety Advisor, Independent Schools Victoria, and former Senior Manager, IB World Schools*

'A wonderful anthology of incidents from a rich teaching experience. I really enjoyed this dip into the quirky, delightful and unexpected world of the primary classroom.'

– John Annable, former teacher and librarian

'From the first page to the last, this collection of funny stories delivers a delightful cocktail of humour and heart. I haven't read many books that managed to strike a perfect balance between raucous amusement and sincere emotion, but this set of tales does so with apparent ease, leaving me both laughing out loud and reflecting quietly on the deeper learnings woven throughout. A fabulous read!'

– Jo Nicholson, teacher, educator and library officer

'Written with clarity, good cheer, and, of course, wit, this book gives us a quick romp through any school. Full of amusing anecdotes and delightful bite-sized stories, it's a joy to read.'

– Janet Muller, educator, and former principal and classroom teacher

*For my students – past, present, and those who still think
the fire alarm is a great way to get out of maths.
Thank you for teaching me patience, resilience, and the
true meaning of chaos. Without your creative interpretations
of instructions, unforgettable show-and-tell performances,
and daily surprises (some requiring immediate evacuation),
this book – and my grey hairs – would not exist.
Here's to the laughter, mischief, and memories we made
together in the wild world of Mr Fav's class!*

*To truly thrive as a teacher, you need three essential qualities:
a wishbone (mostly for hoping you make it to Friday),
a backbone (strong enough to withstand endless meetings),
and a funny bone – because let's be honest,
sometimes the only response is laughter.*

DISCLAIMER

As you flip through these pages, you'll discover that every name has been delightfully scrambled, outrageously reinvented, or plucked straight from the author's wild imagination – sometimes all at once! Here, both heroes and villains are bundled together under the same cosy blanket of anonymity. If you happen to spot a character who seems suspiciously familiar (maybe even a little too much like you), don't worry! It's either a twist of fate, a trick of the literary light, or just your playful mind having some fun. In this topsy-turvy masquerade of made-up names, everyone is equally lost – and just as merrily bewildered – as you are. Enjoy the ride!

CONTENTS

Preface		1
1	King Joe and the Garage of Secrets	3
2	The Sea, the Book, and the Bedroom Blunder	7
3	Secrets, Schedules, and the Snoopy Fourth-Grader	11
4	Jay and the Wild West Angels	13
5	The Stanley Knife That Never Was	15
6	Phonics to the Rescue!	17
7	Spelling Out the Obvious – Tom's Way	19
8	Little Minds, Big Mysteries: The First-Grade Eggsplanation	21
9	Police, Pipes, and Public Oversharing	23
10	Teaching, Taming, and Transit Troubles	25
11	A Sticky Situation: The Case of the Vanishing Adhesive	29
12	Secrets Behind the Dog Flap	31
13	Binoculars, Business, and Brian: The Seal Deal	35
14	Fractions: Hasta La Vista, Whole Numbers	37
15	Billy's Guide to Not Getting Melted	39
16	Say Cheese… and Hope for the Best	41

17	The Day Tom Ran His Own Race	43
18	Sophie's Divine Doodles	45
19	Spinach, Sailors, and Slip-Ups: Olivia's Movie Mix-Up	47
20	The Fast-Forward Approach to NAPLAN Prep	49
21	Lucas and the Literal Search for Answers	51
22	Why Oh Y? Alphabet Antics in Room PF	53
23	Surviving NAPLAN: The Great Aussie Test-a-thon	55
24	Show and Tell or Show and Yell?	57
25	A Ten Out of Ten for Effort	59
26	Spotting Trouble in Prep Orientation	61
27	Wally's Vanishing Act (and My Soaked Heroics)	63
28	When Geometry Gets Heavenly	65
29	Breanna and the Unforgettable Zucchini	67
30	The ABCs of Happily Ever After	69
31	The Great Planet Mix-up	71
32	The Koala Kid Strikes Again	75
33	Anthony's Latest 'Body' of Work	77
34	Jurassic Lark: The Case of the Pilfered Pennies	81
35	Just Another Day in Dob City: The Hearing Scare	85
36	The Fine, Wet Line Between Good and Bad	89
37	Julia's Feathered Fiesta	93
38	The Day the Kids Delivered the F-Bomb	95
39	Aquarium Awkwardness: The Joshua Effect	99
Epilogue		103
About the Author		105

PREFACE

Teaching: less a profession; more an extreme sport played out daily in rooms alive with glitter glue, questionable smells, and unpredictable tiny humans. It's a glorious whirlwind of chaos, surprise, and sheer magic. But for someone who wouldn't trade this wild ride, the sheer volume feels like a creature breeding in the dark corners of my desk.

One moment crafting lessons to ignite curiosity and genuine learning; the next, buried under marking, endless meetings, agonising over report card comments. Add the diplomacy of parent–teacher conferences, and some days my brain feels like it's completed an Olympic decathlon. And yet, in the beautiful eye of this storm, teaching offers a depth of joy and purpose simply unmatched elsewhere.

Let's be honest, the true stars are the students. These pint-sized philosophers, comedians, and accidental scientists consistently keep me wonderfully on my toes. One moment, they're demonstrating Newton's laws with a launched sandwich; the next, they pose a question so profound it makes you blink. Every day feels like a new episode of 'Did That Just Happen?!', packed with laughter, unexpected wisdom, and moments that fundamentally shift your perspective.

Chalk Full of Laughs attempts to capture that electricity. It's a collection of the funniest, most heartwarming, and unforgettable moments witnessed from the classroom front lines. Think of it as a love letter – scribbled in chalk, smudged – to the incredible kids who fill my days with giggles and push me to be a better learner. Teaching is, without question, the best (and undeniably weirdest) job on the planet.

So grab a seat – preferably the one in the back with the secret stash of snacks – and get ready to laugh. Class is officially in session!

1

KING JOE AND THE
GARAGE OF SECRETS

When I first started teaching fourth grade, I expected the usual surprises – forgotten homework, mysterious stains, and at least one child who could burp the alphabet. But nothing could have prepared me for Joe. Picture a pint-sized whirlwind with hair that looked like it had been styled with static electricity and sheer defiance, glasses so enormous they seemed to belong to his future self, and a mouth that never ran out of stories. The minute Joe started talking, the entire class would freeze, spellbound, as if he'd cast a magic spell that made maths worksheets temporarily invisible.

It didn't take long for my students to crown Joe 'The King of Show and Tell'. He took that title seriously, spinning tales so outrageous and detailed that even the classroom goldfish seemed to listen. One epic saga, however, raised the bar to dizzying new heights, unfolding in daily cliff-hangers that had us all on tenterhooks.

Day one, Joe bounced to the front of the class like a caffeinated squirrel. 'Good morning, everyone! You are NOT going to believe what happened!' he declared, pausing dramatically so the suspense had time to marinate. 'Last night, my dad walked in with THREE shiny bikes. One for my brother, one for my sister, and one for ME. And guess what? No birthdays. No Christmas. Just because!' He spread his arms as if he'd single-handedly invented generosity.

'These aren't just any bikes,' he whispered, eyes wide behind his windshield-sized glasses. 'They're Malvern Stars!' He traced invisible frames in the air. 'Six gears that click like a secret agent's gadgets – listen!' (He clicked his tongue for effect.) 'The fenders match the frame, there's a chain guard so your pants don't get gobbled up, and racks on the back for carrying all your stuff!' Around him, awe and envy rippled like a tiny human wave.

Next morning, Joe stumbled in like a miniature zombie, sporting circles under his eyes the size of doughnuts. 'Guys,' he groaned, 'I'm so tired. I was up ALL night playing my brand-new Nintendo!' His exhaustion lasted all of two seconds before he exploded with excitement. 'My dad brought home the biggest colour TV in the store. It's so huge, I think the neighbours across the street can watch our cartoons. Then – boom! – he gives us a Nintendo! I played *Mario* until Mum made me stop. But then…' Joe glanced around, lowering his voice, 'I snuck back after bedtime. Don't tell.' A chorus of gasps and jealous groans followed.

By day three, Joe was practically vibrating in his seat, unable to wait his turn. 'My dad got a Holden Monaro,' he blurted out, leaping up. 'It has GTS racing stripes – like lightning bolts! Makes it go extra fast!' He demonstrated with screeching tyre sounds and invisible gear shifts, earning a round of giggles. Then, he frowned. 'The weird thing is, Dad spent all night painting it. Not sure why. It already looked awesome.'

On the final day, Joe's energy had evaporated. He shuffled to the front, looking as deflated as a forgotten birthday balloon. 'Um, all our new stuff is gone,' he mumbled, scuffing the floor with his shoe. 'Dad moved everything to Grandma's garage last night – the bikes, the TV, the Nintendo, even the Monaro with the racing stripes.' He looked up, eyes puzzled. 'He put a big lock on the door and said not to tell anyone. Because…' Joe hesitated, then shrugged, 'the police are coming over today. I dunno why they want to see our stuff so bad.'

As it turns out, sometimes the real world outshines even Joe's wildest stories – and that's saying something.

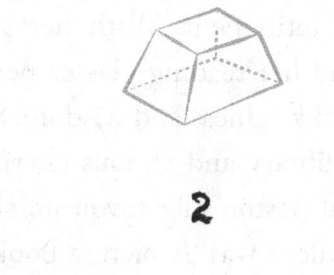

2

THE SEA, THE BOOK, AND THE BEDROOM BLUNDER

A gentle hush settled over the classroom as my prep students finished their work, pencils neatly down and eyes shining with the quiet satisfaction of a job well done. With twenty precious minutes left before their eagerly awaited break, the timing felt ideal for a story – one that would whisk them away on an imaginative adventure.

I glanced around and summoned Charlotte and Clancy, my ever-reliable duo. Their faces lit up, all eager grins and barely contained excitement, as I handed down my special mission. 'Would you please go to the library and ask Mrs Brown for her copy of *There's a Sea in My Bedroom?* I asked, warmth in my voice and hope in my heart.

'Okay!' they sang out together, their little feet tap-tap-tapping joyfully down the corridor, the picture of enthusiasm.

Mrs Brown, our cherished librarian for nearly ten years, was on the brink of retirement. With her silver hair always impeccably pinned and her reading glasses perched just so, she was the embodiment of kindness and wisdom. She split her time between her beloved library and various charitable causes with her husband, the local pastor. Her favourite saying – delivered with a wink and a smile – was 'A picture book a day keeps the cobwebs away.'

Mrs Brown's love for literature shone through in the way she encouraged every child's reading journey, so I was certain she'd know exactly what I needed and would entrust the book to my trusty messengers.

But when the bell shrieked for break and my book-bearers still hadn't returned, a flicker of worry nudged me out of my seat. I hurried to the library, where I found Charlotte and Clancy standing by Mrs Brown, all three turning to me with expectant faces as I entered.

'Mr Fav,' Mrs Brown said, one eyebrow arched in amusement, 'what message did you send with these two?'

I explained, 'I asked them to fetch *There's a Sea in My Bedroom.*' Even as I spoke, a sense of mischief seemed to hover in the air.

Mrs Brown's lips twitched as she suppressed a laugh. 'That's interesting,' she replied, 'because what I heard was "Mr Fav wants to see you in his bedroom."'

The room erupted in laughter, echoing between the shelves. As I tried to recover my composure, I couldn't help but reflect that teaching is 10% inspiration, 15% perspiration, and 75% desperately hoping your instructions don't result in a staffroom scandal.

Meanwhile, Charlotte and Clancy, blissfully unaware of the mix-up, tugged at our sleeves and pleaded, 'Can we go and play now?'

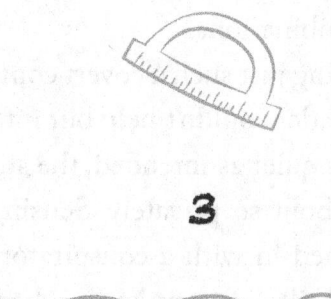

3

SECRETS, SCHEDULES, AND THE SNOOPY FOURTH-GRADER

Planning new class groups is a far more complex operation than just shuffling names around on a chart. We have to strike a careful balance between academic needs, learning styles, unique personalities, behaviour characteristics, traits or patterns, friendship dynamics, who works well together (and, even more crucially, who really doesn't!), parent requests, class sizes, and the ever-perplexing challenge of keeping the gender balance. It's like conducting an orchestra – except sometimes the violins throw tantrums and the flutes have peanut allergies.

Teachers take this job seriously. You'll find us huddled in the corners of the staffroom or whispering in hallways, swapping notes and sharing observations under a veil of confidentiality. These conversations have all the intrigue of a top-secret mission – colleagues popping into each other's classrooms, or lingering after meetings to compare observations and puzzle out the best possible classroom combinations.

One afternoon, during just such a covert conference, a particularly curious fourth-grader couldn't help but interrupt. Eyes wide and voice not nearly as quiet as intended, the student asked what we were whispering about so privately. Sensing an opportunity for a life lesson, I leaned in with a conspiratorial smile and my most meaningful head tilt. 'Do you know what "mind your own business" means?' I asked gently.

The student stared, baffled as if I'd just asked them to explain quantum physics. Before I could develop my heartfelt speech on boundaries and respect, a voice from across the room rang out – loud, clear, and utterly delighted: 'I DO!'

As it turns out, when it comes to curiosity and comic timing, fourth-graders are truly in a league of their own.

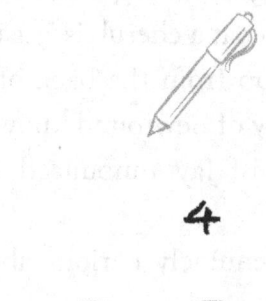

4

JAY AND THE WILD WEST ANGELS

The crisp morning bell echoed across the playground, heralding the start of another bustling school day. Once again, the prep students clung to their parents with tearful embraces and reluctant kisses. They scattered about the asphalt like colourful songbirds, chirping excitedly and fluttering from group to group, tiny fingers reaching out to clasp the hands of familiar friends as they formed their wobbly lines.

Standing before them, I waited with the practised patience of a seasoned teacher, watching as their boundless energy gradually settled. Sunlight streamed through the nearby gum trees, casting dappled shadows across their upturned faces. With a warm smile, I addressed them, 'Good morning, my little cherubs.' Their expressions transformed into masks of adorable confusion, eyebrows furrowed and heads slightly tilted.

'I'm sorry,' I acknowledged, noting their bewilderment, 'but you probably have no idea what a cherub is.' Just as the words left my lips, a small arm shot up from the back of the line, waving with the immediate urgency of newfound knowledge.

'I know what a cherub is!' Jay announced, his voice ringing with confidence.

'Really?' I responded, genuinely curious about what insight this five-year-old might offer.

'Yes!' Jay declared triumphantly, his chest puffing with pride. 'He's the man in charge of the cowboys!'

As I stifled a chuckle, realising he'd likely confused 'cherub' with 'sheriff', I was reminded that teaching is as much about learning from my students as it is about guiding them. Their unique perspectives and unexpected wisdom bring joy and surprise to every day.

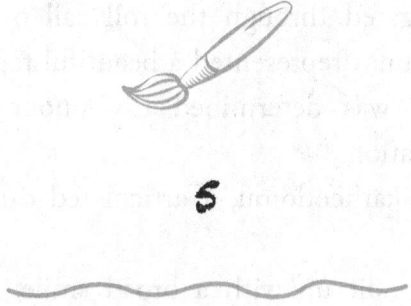

5

THE STANLEY KNIFE THAT NEVER WAS

Mrs Anderson's art room was a sanctuary of order and creativity. Vibrant student masterpieces adorned the walls like a gallery exhibition, each one carefully mounted and displayed.

Every paintbrush, scissor, and coloured pencil was meticulously counted and stored in labelled containers, while work stations gleamed with spotless surfaces and thoughtful organisation.

Fellow teachers were welcome to borrow supplies, provided they followed her detailed sign-out system – a small note indicating name, date, and borrowed item was all she required to maintain her impeccable inventory. Those who dared to flout this simple procedure would inevitably find themselves on the receiving end of Mrs Anderson's determined search for her missing treasures.

On my first day after the sun-drenched summer break, I carefully navigated through the roll call of my new sixth-graders. Their names represented a beautiful tapestry of cultural heritage, and I was determined to honour each one with proper pronunciation.

'Dimitri Patsikatheodorou,' I articulated carefully, savouring each syllable.

The boy's face lit up with a broad smile. 'Good morning, Mr Fav!' he responded with infectious enthusiasm.

'Goran Stojanovski,' I continued, moving down my list.

'Present!' he announced with such volume that it practically echoed off the classroom walls.

'Saoirse Tierney,' I called next, managing the Irish name with confidence.

'Here,' she replied softly, her voice barely carrying across the room.

By the time I finished the roll, I felt a small sense of triumph at having correctly pronounced each student's full given name.

The moment was shattered by three sharp knocks on the door. Mrs Anderson appeared, her head poking through the doorway with an expression of mild concern. 'Do you have a Stanley Knife in this room?' she inquired, her eyes scanning our classroom.

Before I could formulate a response, Goran's voice rang out with absolute certainty: 'No... he's not on our roll!'

Laughter rippled through the class, and I realised once again how quickly order could evaporate – and how, as teachers, we are both the architects and the audience of these unexpected moments.

6

PHONICS TO THE RESCUE!

My first year teaching prep was a whirlwind of vibrant discoveries and heart-warming achievements. I dedicated myself to cultivating warm, respectful bonds with each bright-eyed student, carefully nurturing their budding skills and laying sturdy foundations for their educational journey. The classroom buzzed with laughter and learning, making our inevitable parting at year's end particularly bittersweet.

To celebrate our time together, I organised a festive end-of-year party with colourful decorations and treats. On that final day, my little scholars surprised me with handcrafted cards and thoughtfully wrapped gifts, their faces beaming with pride.

As I opened their precious offerings, emotion overcame me, and tears glistened in my eyes while attempting to read their heartfelt messages.

'I'm sorry,' I managed to say, voice catching. 'It's becoming difficult for me to read through these tears.'

Without missing a beat, one of my practical young pupils exclaimed, 'Just sound it out, Mr Fav!'

In that moment, I realised just how much my students had learned – and how much they had taught me in return.

7

SPELLING OUT THE OBVIOUS – TOM'S WAY

Homework plays an important role in school life – it gives students a chance to practise, build on, and really lock in what they've learned in class. Over the years, I've come up with all sorts of activities: from reading and spelling drills to quick-fire number fact challenges. I even like to mix in tasks that sharpen research skills and get students ready for upcoming tests.

One time, I asked my students to jot down five words they could spell. Tom, ever the literal thinker, handed in his homework with the following list:

1. Five
2. Words
3. You
4. Can
5. Spell.

Honestly, with a sense of humour like that, Tom might just deserve top marks!

8

LITTLE MINDS, BIG MYSTERIES: THE FIRST-GRADE EGGSPLANATION

This timeless riddle has baffled great minds and sparked heated debates for centuries: Which came first: the chicken or the egg? It's a puzzle that circles endlessly, because you need a hen to lay an egg, but every chicken starts its journey inside an egg. It's like a merry-go-round of feathers and fresh starts, with no clear beginning in sight.

One sunny morning, my first-graders and I plopped down in a cosy circle on the classroom carpet, ready to tackle this age-old mystery together. I tossed the question into the air, and the room fell into a hush, little brows furrowing with deep concentration.

Then, in the middle of the silence, a tiny hand shot up as if propelled by rocket fuel.

'Egg!' Isabelle announced, her voice brimming with the unshakeable confidence only a first-grader can muster.

Trying not to grin, I nudged her for more. 'And how do you know it's the egg, Isabelle?'

She didn't hesitate for an instant – her answer was as quick as a crack of an eggshell: 'Eggs are for breakfast, and chicken is for dinner!'

I couldn't help but laugh. 'Fair point! But tell me, where do our eggs come from?'

Without missing a beat, Isabelle delivered her final fridge-worthy logic: 'From the fridge of course!'

And just like that, the mystery was solved – at least until lunchtime.

9

POLICE, PIPES, AND PUBLIC OVERSHARING

The Police Schools Involvement Program was created with two main goals: to educate students about the challenges and responsibilities they will encounter as they grow up, and to close the often uncomfortable gap between young people and the police. The program also aimed to help students see officers as supportive members of the community, rather than just people who issue speeding tickets or respond to minor complaints.

Given how many temptations seem to lurk around every teenage corner – some legal, some not so much – it's no surprise that drug education became a centre-piece of the program. The idea was to scare us straight, or at least get us thinking twice before accepting any 'weird candy' from strangers.

There's one particular afternoon that's forever burned into my brain. Two officers, looking both friendly and faintly intimidating in their crisp uniforms, strode into our sixth-grade classroom. They carried with them an assortment of mysterious objects meant to shock us into making good choices. Among these artefacts was a real-life meth pipe, which they brandished like Indiana Jones showing off a cursed relic.

The whole class leaned forward, equal parts horrified and fascinated. And then, just as the officers paused for dramatic effect, a voice piped up from the back of the room: 'Hey! My dad has one of those!' Instantly, the temperature in the room seemed to drop ten degrees. The officers stared at each other in panic, probably wishing they could vanish into thin air. Before anyone could say a word, the boy's friend hissed, 'Luke! Do you want to get your dad arrested?'

We all learned a lesson that day – about drugs, about timing, and about the importance of not over-sharing in public. But if anyone learned the most, it was definitely Luke.